I WAS WAITING TO SEE WHAT YOU WOULD DO FIRST

Miller Williams Poetry Series
EDITED BY BILLY COLLINS

I WAS WAITING
TO SEE
WHAT
YOU
WOULD
DO FIRST

POEMS BY ANGIE MAZAKIS

The University of Arkansas Press
Fayetteville
2020

Copyright © 2020 by The University of Arkansas Press

ISBN: 978-1-68226-134-7
eISBN: 978-1-61075-691-4

24 23 22 21 20   5 4 3 2 1

Designed by Liz Lester

⊗ The paper used in this publication meets the minimum requirements of
the American National Standard for Permanence of Paper for Printed Library
Materials Z39.48-1984.

Library of Congress Cataloging-in-Publication Data

Names: Mazakis, Angie, author.
Title: I was waiting to see what you would do first / poems by Angie Mazakis.
Description: Fayetteville : The University of Arkansas Press, 2020. |
    Series: Miller Williams poetry series | Summary: "These poems explore
    place, family of origin, and fractured time through expansive lines and
    settings that challenge a reader's sense of perception. A finalist for
    the 2020 Miller Williams Poetry Prize, this work was selected by series
    editor Billy Collins"— Provided by publisher.
Identifiers: LCCN 2019053479 (print) | LCCN 2019053480 (ebook) |
    ISBN 9781682261347 (paperback) | ISBN 9781610756914 (ebook)
Subjects: LCGFT: Poetry.
Classification: LCC PS3613.A974 I19 2020 (print) | LCC PS3613.A974
    (ebook) | DDC 811/.6—dc23
LC record available at https://lccn.loc.gov/2019053479
LC ebook record available at https://lccn.loc.gov/2019053480

CONTENTS

When the University of Arkansas Press invited me to be the editor of its annual publication prize named in honor of Miller Williams—the long-time director of the press and its poetry program—I was quick to accept. Since 1988, when he published my first full-length book, *The Apple that Astonished Paris,* I have felt keenly indebted to Miller. Among the improvements to the world made by Miller before his death in January 2015 at the age of eighty-four was his dedication to finding a place for new poets on the literary stage. In 1990, this commitment became official when the first Arkansas Poetry Prize was awarded. Fittingly, upon his retirement, the prize was renamed the Miller Williams Poetry Prize.

When Miller first spotted my poetry, I was forty-six years old with only two chapbooks to my name. Not a pretty sight. Miller was the one who carried me across that critical line, where the "unpublished poets" impatiently wait, and who made me, in one stroke, a "published poet." Funny, you never hear "unpublished novelist." I suppose if you were a novelist who remained unpublished you would stop writing novels. Not the case with many poets, including me.

Miller Williams was more than my first editor. Over the years, he and I became friends, but even more importantly, before I knew him, I knew his poems. His straightforward, sometimes folksy, sometimes witty, and always trenchant poems were to me models of how poems might sound and how they could *go.* He was one of the poets who showed me that humor had a legitimate place in poetry—that a poem could be humorous without being silly or merely comical. He also showed me that a plain-spoken poem did not have to be imaginatively plain or short on surprises. He was one of my literary fathers.

Miller occupied a solid position on the American literary map, though considering his extensive career and steady poetic output, it's surprising that his poems don't enjoy even more prominence. As his daughter became the well-known singer and recording artist that she is today, Miller came to be known as the father of Lucinda Williams. Miller and Lucinda even appeared on stage together several times, performing a father-daughter act of song and poetry. In 1997, Miller came to the nation's attention when Bill Clinton chose him to be the inaugural poet at his second inauguration. The poem he wrote for that day, "Of History and Hope," is a meditation on how "we have memorized America." In turning to the children of our country, he broadens a nursery rhyme question by asking "How does *our* garden grow?" Miller knew that occasional poems, especially for occasions of such importance, are notoriously difficult—some would say impossible—to write with success. But he rose to that occasion and produced a winner. His confident reading of the poem before the nation added cultural and emotional weight to the morning's ceremony and lifted Miller Williams to a new level of popularity and respect.

Miller was pleased by public recognition. What poet is immune? At home one evening, spotting a headline in a newspaper that read POET BURNS TO BE HONORED, Miller's wife Jordan remarked "They sure have your number." Of course, it was the day dedicated annually to honoring Robert Burns.

Miller's true legacy lies in his teaching and his career as a poet, which covered four decades. In that time, he produced over a dozen books of his own poetry and literary theory. His poetic voice tends to be soft-spoken but can be humorous or bitingly mordant. The poems sound like speech running to a meter. And they show a courteous, engaging awareness of the presence of a reader. Miller knew that the idea behind a good poem is to make the reader feel something, rather than to merely display the poet's emotional state, which has a habit of boiling down to one of the many forms of misery. Miller also possessed the authority of experience to produce poems that were just plain wise.

With Miller's sensibility in mind, I set out to judge the first year's contest. I was on the lookout for poems that resembled Miller's. But the more I read, the more I realized that applying such narrow criteria would be selling Miller short and not being fair to the entrants. It would make more sense to select manuscripts that Miller would enjoy reading for their own merits, not for their similarity to his own poems. That his tastes in poetry were broader than the territory of his own verse can be seen in the variety of the books he published. The list included poets as different from one another as John Ciardi and Jimmy Carter. Broadening my own field of judgment brought happy results, and I'm confident that Miller would enthusiastically approve of this year's selections, as well as those in previous years.

The poems in Jayson Iwen's *Roze & Blud,* winner of the 2020 Miller Williams Poetry Prize, are split into two sections, with a change of speakers in between. First Roze Mertha speaks, then William Blud. Iwen, the poet giving this pair the powers of speech, is a distant literary cousin of Robert Browning, for both poets are interested in how the human character—soul, really—reveals itself in speech. Get someone to talk long enough and the truth about them will be known.

Roze's poems enter without knocking. Here are a few of her opening lines: "They shouldn't let men as young and beautiful / as Mr. Fiedler teach high school." "I love the smell of fabric softener on the breeze." "How can a boy as dumb as Ash Reed / make someone like me horny?" "I live with my real dad in a trailer park / on a ridge above town, / and Mom's already on her third husband, over in Wisconsin now." The subtle "town / now" rhyme in that last quote along with an ability to reflect on the bedrock themes of the beauty and the brevity of life hints at a poetic maturity that emerges as we wade deeper into her poems. Roze's downhome, earthy voice arises from her life in a "shitty little beautiful / trailer park." Her world, which smells of "Old Spice and cigarettes," is part of the familiar landscape of rural American poverty where the young die by drugs, car crashes, or their own hands. Iwen dodges the inherent dangers of sentimentality and anger by giving Roze a straightforward, authentic voice. She doesn't decry her disadvantaged life; she personifies it. A friend "dropped acid in the park / and woke up on Broadway." "Whenever neighbor Angie went on a bender, I knew / because her kids weren't at the bus stop in the morning." Through the natural cadence of her talk, Roze invites us into her life without making any more or less of it than it is.

Somewhere in this procession of poems, a shift occurs and Roze's language becomes almost unintentionally poetic. She "can hear the Berlin Wall falling" in the voice of a boy rocker. She can also hear "a church bell echoing / in the ruins of a city." As she becomes more reflective, the poems turn into existential meditations on the same obsessions that drove the poems of Keats or Yeats. Here's a sample: "We could go on into the unknown / and completely forget one another / until one distant day / we smell tomato soup and tuna / and think, Oh my god / that smells like something I ate / when I was in love." This group of linked poems leads to no conclusion other than Roze's maturation. Roze stares directly into some terrible truths (she calls pain "our final companion") but her final lines contain a limited hopefulness as she imagines the dead who will "die again in us / rise again in us."

William Blud, a former boxer and an aging Vietnam veteran, has graduated from the school of hard knocks. "I've known the intimacy of the world / mostly by blows, rib by broken rib / nose by broken nose." Shrapnel is buried "like treasure inside" him. An apparent victim of PTSD, he is haunted by memories not just of war but his childhood. "I awoke to the familiar sound / of artillery in the distance / but I lay on a soft bed. / Diaphanous blue drapes / rose and settled and rose again." He accepts the diagnosis: "It is a terrible condition, I know / but I am told it is only temporary, / that only the horizon endures." He is a man leaning against a lamppost in the rain, soaking wet; a man waiting for a friend under an overpass; a man who visits children's graves in a cemetery; a creature of winter; a kind of last-man-standing who is left to elegies about his dead friends and his dead wife, Mary. He has empathy for the animal world, a fondness for walking, and enough remaining grit and a bitter sense of irony to end his elegy for Mary with "I don't need to tell you / I always hated that cat. / There, I said it again." A vein of self-pity runs through these poems, but that is true to the aim of the dramatic monologue: to reveal character, no matter what. If the path of young Roze lies ahead of her, the path of William Blud lies behind him. Full of regret and sadness, he is best left with this alert apprehension in an empty parking lot "where a fox stands in the falling snow, / and nothing else moves / but the bouquets of breath / taken from us by the breeze. / The fox watches me, and I watch it. Neither of us will move / until one of us moves."

The poems in Judy Halebsky's *Spring and a Thousand Years (Unabridged)*, finalist for the 2020 Miller Williams Poetry Prize, exist in a state of paradox, the speaker of this collection being poised between contemporary American culture and a China that is both geographically and chronologically remote. One foot is in the familiar world of bike rides to the movies and "T-back tankinis;" the other is planted in the world evoked by Chinese poetry, which speaks in the language of "moon," "nest," and "wing beats." At several points, Halebsky seeks to bridge these two realms by writing letters to Li Bai, the eighth century poet known also as Li Po. The epistolary approach underscores the sharp contrasts between the two spaces and eras. The results are sometimes humorous as the poet tries to explain the oddness of American life: "They sell beer in cans . . . I know, it's amazing."

At other points Li Bai, who "wants to meet Robert Hass," and his fellow poetry master Du Fu are teleported (why not?) into their future / our present, where they smoke cigarettes, ask about Charles Wright (not the one who sings "Express Yourself"), and play cards with a deck that's missing an ace. All this chronological play produces some jarring moments as when Li Bai orders a bourbon in a karaoke bar. Such moments come off as playful skits, but as a whole, this book is guided by serious intent. The environment is not ignored. Whales are disappearing. The globe's waters are rising.

Halebsky's stylistic range is on full display when she switches from pure observation (moon, water) to a kind of revved up American rap. This is how she likes her free verse: "I want it big like a cherry Slurpee, a boob job in an anime film, the biceps of a trainer at Gold's Gym. Bursting, pushing on prose, veering toward some movie script with popcorn and hair-salon updos and all the hours until dawn." In lesser words, she likes the unleashed energy of poetry, and in the poems gathered here, she delivers.

There seems to be no such thing as a typical poem by Angie Mazakis, whose collection *I Was Waiting to See What You Would Do First* is also a finalist for the 2020 Miller Williams Poetry Prize, mostly because this book is bursting with variations in form and sensibility. But here is a clue:

> The newspaper says,
> "Woman in Iceland
> Unknowingly Joins
> Search for Herself."
> She heard her own
> description and it was
> a resemblance she
> couldn't imagine, long
> eraser strokes softening
> her temples, eyes drawn too

wide. She said *"No one ever*
discovers me," and even when
she blew her own *cover*
she was *missed.*

On display here are an attraction to oddities and a fondness for paradoxes, especially ones that collapse on top of each other. What follows those lines is "When I look / at a missing girl's / child photo, I don't know her, / but I feel like only / I know the nuances in her / face." Many of these poems present a provisional narrative which, by the end of the poem, is overwhelmed with asides. Mazakis tirelessly shuttles back and forth between the mind and the world, the psyche and the bus stop, creating a perfect mix of clarity and mystery. She seems to be as fascinated by the external world as she is by her internal life. Her most arresting insights occur when she allows herself to be distracted, or better still, when she becomes the distraction, then vanishes with it under her arm. The attention demanded from the reader by these poems is exhilarating.

Shifting planes of reality and intention make up much of the imaginative play here. In a poem titled "I Miss the Friday Train and Have to Take the Monday Train," we accept the suspension or disappearance of the weekend, but other entities slide in and out of focus as well. "Once I unexpectedly saw a person I loved in my hometown, and then my hometown was no longer my hometown, just a place he was and then wasn't anymore." Another poem is presented like a movie, that is, scene by scene, but here the scenes repeat or contradict one another, and characters walk "out of the frame" and reappear as extras. Turn the page and a love affair is mixed together with the predicament of a couple stuck on Everest, running out of oxygen. There's a poem consisting only of quotes from the TV show *Hoarders*. A favorite of mine titled "Aircraft Safety Information Pamphlet," begins,

The cartoon guy lifting the raft has one hand
resting on his knee like this is old hat, this
releasing the raft from the aircraft.
He's been rafting before.

Such helpful titles and formal patterning give the reader just enough reality to hang on to as Mazakis takes us on a freedom ride of associations, droll reflections, and strange observations. We know where we are going, then we don't. We are quickly moved from expectation to surprise and back again. And to entice you, here are a few of many local delights "We've agreed not to appear in each other's dreams" and "I make a face like I see someone I know outside the train, but they can't see inside." Finally, in a poem titled "Illusions of Self-Motion," lies this lovely speculation on the consequences of gravity increasing in strength: "You pull gravity in close, / the stars compressing until Orion's cloak falls to earth." There are no apparent limits to the imaginative reach of Angie Mazakis.

Congratulations to all three of these poets. The press is honored to be the home for these titles for years to come.

Billy Collins

for my parents, Richard Winston and Jean Mazakis

The first anatomists likened the brain,
pulp and rind, to an orange.
Its beginnings are a mulberry of cells,
and all desire and despair
are seeded in its un- and in-foldings.

—RONALD JOHNSON, Ark

I WAS WAITING TO SEE WHAT YOU WOULD DO FIRST

Oh My Kidneys

In a suburb outside of Chicago, my parents
sit next to each other at their respective dialysis machines.
Outside, the trees aren't touching each other.

My mom says she never feels her blood
leaving her body or entering after it's dialyzed.
If only we could feel what didn't work inside us

as it moves out of us—our illusions, misperceptions,
the heartlessness within the heart. In the 80s, my grandma
would sit on our sofa and watch, on the news, bombs falling

on Beirut, missiles landing in her neighborhood: "Oh my
kidneys," she'd say, because that's what she heard when
people here said "oh my goodness."

My dad first knew he needed glasses when he was standing
on a landing in his family's apartment building in West
Beirut during the War of 1958; he couldn't see the gun

pointing at him from the building across the street.
His mother pushed him out of the way and took him to the
eye doctor the next day. When my uncle tried to correct

my grandmother, so she'd finally say "oh my goodness,"
my dad told her, "He doesn't know English." His
nephrologist keeps telling him to stop skipping dialysis.

"Your kidneys are shit," was the latest diagnosis
from an ER doctor. "They've bottomed out."
"Oh my kidneys," says my dad.

My brother asks my dad if he can take the standing globe
my dad has had for so long that it still says Palestine on it.
He says, "Take it." I buy a globe that lights up

at a thrift store and offer it to my dad. He holds up his hand,
and says, "No, I'm tired of the world." I lied.
My parents each go to different dialysis centers in different

suburbs of Chicago, but whenever I picture them they're
together. Or I want to picture them together. They finally
have something in common. What are the chances?

The last year that my mom could still walk on her own,
could still drive her own car, I was on the phone with her;
she was lost in one of the suburbs near Chicago.

She was supposed to see houses, but instead she saw water
and trees. "I went the wrong way," she said,
"and the wrong way is beautiful."

I put the last piece of namoura cake in my dad's mouth,
but he says he can't taste the same way anymore. He can't
taste the orange blossom water. "I can taste it," he says,

"but it's way far away, like we're still walking toward it."

Love and Containment

I shift and contain varieties of awareness, in an almost subconscious moment when I try to perceive Eve the way Loni, who I haven't seen in three years, might perceive her.

Caroline finds a single hair on her skirt as she sits in the backseat on the way to a party, and does not want to just throw it, imposingly, on the floor of Christine's car.

Stacy could be described as a collection of rice paper boxes, feather baskets, linen envelopes sealed with thread; she locates and contains every subtle distinction then packages and insulates with sympathetic curiosity.

When I go to sit next to six-year-old Sarah, she cups her hands around the portion of the pillow that is a shade darker, to protect me from lying there.

Eve says she couldn't sleep for an entire week. So, when her eyes finally closed for more than a moment, and the construction crew outside began drilling into the concrete, Matt gently placed his hands over her ears.

As I maneuver through the crowd in the living room, on my way to the porch, my hand feels utterly unheld.

"My tears are all right here," says little Sarah.

Caroline does not want to impose even the softest, frailest burden on the car floor.

When I return to the porch, Stacy has her hand lightly cupped over the top of my soda. "I didn't want anything to get in there," she says.

The act of lifting hair from fabric should be assigned a unique word. A word softer than *pulling* or *picking* which more accurately describe extracting something firmly fixed. More vivid than *getting*. A word that indicates easy delay, the faint resistance of static. And then this word, because of its diaphanous sound, would be a homonym for the small moment that little Sarah altered the position of her hand, so slightly, to more accurately quarantine her tears. Both meanings would bear the implication of an unhurried tenderness.

I would enjoy this party food more, I think, had it all been arranged inside plastic eggs.

Sometime before we arrive at the party, while Elena and Lindsay are inevitably already talking about a guy named Bronson—how he always says the wrong thing, will still be talking about him long after we arrive—I watch

Caroline, in the back seat, privately tilting her purse toward her, opening it, and putting one delicate hair inside.

Every Miss Universe Contestant Is from Earth

Your qualifications are that you watched
so many Ice Bucket Challenge videos without
anyone knowing, just so you could hear
people's voices you hadn't heard in ten years.
You've discovered a new way of listening
so that every other sound hurts you.
Everyone who destroyed you thought
They had acted just fine according
to the Geneva Convention or whatever, until
you were left speaking only
in spondees: Wait here. Don't go. Find me.

People like you, because you awaken
the old abuse they knew, and they're
nostalgic. Your talent is to find those
who can identify the widowmaker
part of the heart without an ultrasound.
Your talent is to lose
track of the moment in the story
that people deeply protest. Your talent
is to tuck unscreams and anti-gasps
beneath connective tissue until each
muscle is an arrow pulled back in the bow.
Your platform is "Pretending
like nothing happened"
and "Who I would have been."

Dreamsickness

An expansive, manicured lawn in an uncharted suburb covered all
in shadow like the sun has just set or never existed there will incite a
feeling of distance, will ferment inside you inside your dream, the trees
only pine and paper birch. *Beauty is symmetry is a lie,* we said, eventually.
But it's the lie of the beholder, someone answered. Loneliness can destroy
the quality of sleep. At times, the dream could more accurately be
called a distance. Do you make facial expressions in your dreams? You
can't tell. A mysterious sleeping sickness is causing hundreds of people
in a small town near a former Soviet Union uranium mine to sleep
for days and wake up with significant memory loss. The doctors who
have been flown in do not know why. They ruled out everything one
by one while we were crossing destinations off a dream map. We've
agreed not to appear in each other's dreams. Inflammation, learning
and memory deficits, high blood pressure, hardening of the arteries
are some of the illnesses caused by loneliness. You remember that
earlier in the dream, three dreams into the night's long sequence of
dreams, you made someone cry, and you ran after them to make it
right and chased them into a crowd and lost them for the rest of the
dream, which in the dream was the rest of your life. Loneliness is as
deadly as lack of exercise, as some terminal illnesses. Do not let the
open landscape of your dreams induce the terror of possibility, the
anticipation of openness unfolding into emptiness; the wide corridors
of a hospital are part of a therapeutic design to dissuade a fight-or-
flight response. Floor-to-ceiling windows and skylights help encourage
adaption to biological rhythms to accelerate healing. Walk into the
open space and picture a point beyond it that opens it further, a point
beyond that, and so on until it opens all the way and you find yourself
on the other side, awake. You imagine every sleeping person in that
Soviet town trying to pinch themselves awake in their dreams. You've
heard of people trying to pinch themselves awake, but what good
would your dreamed hands be, validating your own momentary,
muted, dreamed skin?

Illusions of Self-Motion

Can you bind the beautiful Pleiades?
Can you loose the cords of Orion?

—JOB 38:31

Illusory movements of a person's entire body
or of individual limbs can occur when no movement
is actually occurring. You may feel your hand
move to take another hand, for example,
though your arm remains at your side. It is possible
but rare, that one may feel one's own heart
plunge below sea level where it cannot beat,
but where it is immersed silently, its own stillness
deliciously painful, the way drowning is rumored to be,
as a quiet sickness grows within it. In fact, the heart
has remained stationary in the body all along.
It is almost unheard of to feel the movement
of memory through its various iterations and final expulsion—
the mind's varied attempts to pacify move transiently.
It is rare, but when this movement is felt, it manifests as falling
just before waking.

In subjective vertigo, a person feels their own body
moving when it is not moving. They may feel
themselves being pulled relentlessly one way.
Such as seaward, or homeward, or heavenward, or toward
a small appliances sale. Toward the very thing that is hurting,
humiliating you. Resist the desire to make gravity work
harder, to ask it to help you trust it, pull its weight
around here. You will want it to grow stronger.
If it were stronger, the stars would grow larger,
denser, closer together—cells moving to form a malignant

mass and nothing can stop it. Planets orbiting the stars
would have to travel faster. Their manifold suns, having lost
all patience, howling, *Now see what you've made me do?*
would toss the planets around wildly. First, close your eyes
and empty the earth; look around and try to see the landscape
without evidence of anyone having lived there. Try this deep
into the night, beyond midnight, past a measure of time
that is familiar to us. To find this, go to the intimation
of the perimeter of emptiness. Listen closely; you can hear
where it ends—the sound of water on tin, an isolated metronome,
keeping a solitary time apart from any measure we've known.

When a train or car approaches or departs,
a person who experiences linear vection feels
as though their body has advanced or moved in reverse
rather than the vehicle. The emptiness fills you
and exhausts you, accuses you of being
small in the universe—all of us becoming
smaller as the universe expands, so that all our pictures
will soon be nailed to telephone poles. The first face
I see is so delicate, that her features are barely there
to begin with. In the parking lot, the car next to me moves,
and I think my car is moving, so I drop my phone.
Astronomers have long known that young stars
could be found near the center of the galaxy,
but they had no idea how they got there.
We caught these stars in the act
of forming.

A pilot executing a coordinated turn will have no awareness
of their motion in the air without a discernable horizon.
You just see one moment; you just see now. There is nothing
ahead of you or behind you. You pull gravity in close,
the stars compressing until Orion's cloak falls to earth.
When others come straight through, you are standing
a little to the side for them. Eventually the planets
would be torn apart and swallowed into one of the stars.
When you notice the expanse of earth, it feels as though
you've been called the wrong name; no one remembers you;
someone has connected the stars an alternate way to make
entirely new constellations—one in the shape of
the alternative to your existence.

People with No Sight Still See Ghosts

a news story headline

It's not the feeling of wind but of trying to feel wind
on a still day, and suddenly you're a kite-flyer, a sailor;
the wind's potential direction and speed are necessary;
how far and fast will you have to follow
what could be swiftly taken away.
A blind man who gained his sight saw people
walking away as *inexplicably shrinking*.
I was walking my friend's dog, and it was barking
at nothing; it was barking at the light disappearing into the clouds.
I was trying to decide who to tell an important thing first,
so I could say, *You're the only person I've told.*
I looked inside someone's house and could see inside
a window and then inside their French doors, where
someone with hands on both handles opened them outward.
Historically, French doors opened inward,
and so did you, for a while. Then you shrank inexplicably
from me, and I followed the light through the opening
in the door as long as I could. I put my finger on it
and followed it until I could no longer see it,
and then I was accidentally pointing at a hot air balloon
that you could have maybe seen from where you were
until it curved around whichever way the
trade winds blew.
Before everyone believed the earth was round, some knew that
it was round, because if you stood on the seashore and watched
a ship sailing away, it would disappear from view, but if you climbed
to a higher point—a hill or a tower, the ship would become visible
again. And when it vanished again, the hull vanished first, and then

the sails and smokestack disappeared last, as though the ship
was dropping behind a hill.
Once, the wind blew right through all the holes
in your heart, and the sound was 40 low notes blown
into glass bottles.
Once, I found your whisper
on a wind map.

I Am Looking for You Here

I.

I remember walking down the street in Haifa
with my sister Teresa, being chased
by a rooster. I don't remember what
happened, how we got away. It's like
being chased in a dream and you wake up
before you find out how it ends.

When I ask about my dad's first memory
of Palestine, I drink Arab coffee
until the silt that remains is wet
sand collected in a pail.
There is no word in Arabic for *consistency.*

I tell him that last week I received
a message from a stranger:
"We have the same last name.
Are we related? My father was born
in West Jerusalem, fled to Jordan."

I leave olives on my plate and
think about them being picked
from the same tree, sent to different
factories, packed in separate jars,
then finding their way in another
country to the same dish. He says:

While we drove from Haifa to Beirut,
My father wore a fedora through the Jewish areas,
And through the Arab areas, he wore a fez,

As I sift my fork through the rice, I try
to extract all the French out of his Arabic.

When there was shooting
we hid in the neighbor's house.
In the inside room.

I remember my
father screamed: "Leave everything.
We are coming back."

II.

I am eleven in Indiana at my dad's
Arab restaurant, and I know
that if I keep my eyes on the shelves,
the jars of olives and grape leaves,
and listen to my dad yelling Arabic
at the cooks, I can imagine that I am
in Jerusalem or Bethlehem, that he never
left, that we have just shared mangoes
from his neighbor's tree. Then I hear
my own voice asking for apples in English,
and I am back in Indiana, where there
is a word for *privacy*.

"And there is no word is Arabic for *to miss*,
like *to miss someone?*" I ask. "So, what
did you say when you were here
in America and you missed your family?"

In Arabic, we say, I am looking for you
here, but I can't find you.

III.

The birthplace on his passport is
a place he has never heard of.
"We do not recognize Palestine,"
they told him, "in America."
His birthplace on his passport
is a place that is uninhabited.
There is no word in Arabic for *is*.

They told me that when I was three,
I was at my grandmother's house,
eight blocks away. Winding roads, not like here.
My mother heard me outside, calling her name.
I was three years old and I found my way back
through eight blocks of winding roads.
I found my way home.
I don't remember this, though.
It is only what I was told.

There's No Face for This

When I heard that Inge's dad died, immediately his face
was the face of the main character in the book I was reading, and
the character inherited his face for the rest of the book.

Inge's dad died of a heart attack; the dad in the book was a devout
jogger, so the character had a new insistent mortality each time he
was red-faced, running. The face I pictured as the jogger's daughter

was not Inge; instead I imagined the daughter as the girl who, in real life,
told me when I was eight that if you chew on celery long
enough, it turns into gum, which never worked but which I still

try sometimes, and she taught me how to sing in close harmony
just by listening to her, like incidentally adopting a new facial
expression you barely noticed. Even though she was nothing like

the main character's daughter, her face fit the character better than
it fit her. The song that's come on the radio will always remind me
of the year I left the rolling hills, which wasn't a bad year,

but was a year of looking back upon a bad year. It was the year
that faces stopped coinciding axiomatically with emotion, and you
had to exert the deliberate effort to make your face match each

spontaneous, conscious emotion. The mechanism had been
dismantled, implicit memory impaired. Our feelings staggered
behind our faces, missed their targets. The way deer need two

senses to determine danger, the emotion coordinate had to meet
with the facial muscle coordinate to equal an expression. In my
mind, I used my hands to connect them every time. If you felt

a complex medley of emotions, you had to express them
in a succession of appropriate singular expressions and gestures.
Which took some time and made everything in life longer.

If you felt an emotion for which we had no specific identifiable
expression, you made that face that had no specific identifiable
expression. Which is the face most people make most of the time

and which was not far off from a face of resignation or the face that
said, "It's too hard to make a face for this." Jobs were lost, because
people made the wrong or confusing faces in most work

environments, because, while before, deliberately making a face
that was disconnected to your emotions was common in the
workplace, now that it was required, everyone either rebelled,

displaying their emotions dramatically, or they couldn't get their
faces to make a face that said, "I'm so sorry the boss is taking a year-
long leave of absence." However, jobs were created as well, because

people had a hard time manually coordinating faces with emotions,
so they hired facial expression coaches. My coach proved unhelpful,
but when I tried to make a face that said, "You're fired," I made

a face that said, "I'm hungry," which I knew because he'd held out
for me an apple. So, I kept him as a coach, because I couldn't make
that face, and I certainly couldn't say it.

One day, leaving his office, I saw you in your coat, walking along the
old main street. I'd completely changed my appearance, so I didn't
recognize you at all at first. I wasn't facing toward or away from you,

but at an angle that nevertheless identified you peripherally. Before I could even see your face, I made a face that said, "I've forgotten," but I made it too soon, and it wouldn't come again when I tried.

I lifted my hands and then put them down again, and at that moment, I felt that I'd lost the ability to show any emotion through touching someone as well, and I kept squeezing my hands into each

other to get it going again. When you turned toward me, I made the face that said, "I don't feel alone," which is the same face that says, "Winter is coming," even if it isn't, and surprisingly the same face

that says, "I can't find my driver's license." You made a face that asked something (and faces that asked were the hardest to make unaided), but you didn't ask anything. Then I made a face that said,

"There aren't enough background noises here," and then, "This is the face my face makes without you," and then accidentally and out of turn a face that said, "Inge's dad died." Which is the same face

for, "Please walk away now," which you did, and which didn't matter, I guess, because then I just kept making, over and over, not a face that didn't say anything, but a face that said, "Nothing."

Index of Continuity Errors

First, you were in the background laughing,
then when we saw you a second
later, you were abruptly not laughing.

An establishing scene revealed your coat
hanging in the closet, deliberately part of the set,
then later it was just gone.

In one sequence, my drink was low.
In the next shot it was full again, and in
 every shot after, I kept drinking,
and it was still full.

I crossed the axis of action—the invisible line
which maintains the space between us—
disrupting the predictable trajectory of the narrative.

(You walked out of the frame.
Then the timeskip three years later
showed you walking into the background
wearing a face from some ancient tragedy
we lack the coarse and underived
receptivity to make now.)

There were only supposed to be two people
in the frame, but if a viewer looked closely
at the reflection in the car door in the alley
during the cutaway, a third person could be seen
whom no one was supposed to see.

In one scene you were leaving through the front door,
and a split edit revealed two people whispering,

then the shot showed you leaving
through the front door again.

A still frame caused you to appear sympathetic,
but we know that you weren't actually capable
of demonstrating sympathy until possibly several
years after this scene or maybe never.

Our reactions and gestures were
bullet holes in the wall before shots were fired.

Your heart was totaled in one scene—two
visible gashes, several considerable dents,
but when you walked out of the frame and back in
a minute later, it was back together again
in one piece, while mine was still visibly wrecked.

In a later scene, some stranger who represented
possibility walked toward me, stage left, and
I was like the boy in *North by Northwest*, who,
before the gunshot rang out, knew to cover his ears.

Aircraft Safety Information Pamphlet

The cartoon guy lifting the raft has one hand
resting on his knee like this is old hat, this
releasing the raft from the aircraft.
He's been rafting before.

The woman waiting to get on the raft is leaning
back on one leg; she knows that even in an escape,
things take time, so, might as well relax.

This is the most casual escape in the history of escapes.

There is a mountain near them, in the background,
which makes the cartoon passengers think,
Look how narrowly we escaped that mountain.

The woman leaning back on one leg looks as though
maybe her illustrator drew her with a cigarette in her hand,
at first, and then his boss said *Stop dinking around, Bill.*

Another woman is demonstrating that you should help yourself
before you help others, and now she's fastening the air mask
on her little boy, which is just cruel, because children should not be
exposed to hypothetical tragedies, when you can prevent it
by just not drawing them into one.

A woman is about to head down the emergency slide,
and the man standing behind her is leaning against the emergency
exit and has obviously just said something like, *You're going
to want a man to do this*, before pushing her aside.
But it's an emergency, so she lets it slide—*Emergency slide,*
she thinks, with an annoyed face in the next panel
as she's heading down the chute.

The cartoon survivors are all wearing khaki slacks
and a nice button-down or suits and skirts, which says
that *anything can happen*, even to professional businesspeople.

It means that if they don't succeed in operating
the door hatch or releasing the oxygen mask,
they will leave behind, at the very least,
unfinished annual reports and God
knows how many solicited business proposals.

There are, optimistically, two surviving groups of people.
One on each side of the plane.

Everyone gets out.

And they float safely away for any number of days
on Bill's deadline-rushed drawing of a capable raft.

The Woman Who Lives inside My GPS
Directs Her Thoughts Inward

Often while I'm telling you to take the next legal U-turn, and you're looking for a way around it, my mind drifts far beneath sea level to the battles for survival going on there.

I like to imagine that I'm completely lost.

I've always dreamed of creating a new font, and my voice would sound like that. Soft but alert. Like the violin notes that begin the third movement of Rimsky-Korsokov's *Scheherazade*.

I was born without any grandparents and almost entirely without a sense of urgency.

When people are driving, they wear all the faces of a tense conversation, but no words come out.

I see directions as shapes. The route from your house to Walgreens is a bird's beak.

I see shapes in the filigree tiles in my bathroom. Today, a bull's face.

My own face has a familiarity I can't place.

My sister and I had the same capabilities, but she had larger hopes.

She once thought of devoting her life to following a single penny through every exchange.

Don't treat me like I'm a genie trapped in here; this is just my job.

When I use my own GPS, it can't be in my voice. I can't stomach the sound.

It sounds as though I'm really concentrating, but I can do this with my eyes closed. I take you over the Dan Ryan to I–294, make you pay all the tolls, while I am drinking peach sparkling water in bed and taking an "Are You a Sociopath?" quiz online.

53% sociopath, it says.

One joke I hate is when people say I *get around*.

I go out with my friends, and they call me a late bloomer. I really haven't been that many places.

Sometimes mine is the only voice speaking, but I'm still easy to ignore, I guess.

There are so many words in my head that I don't say you. Mainly, *Just trust me* and *Not yet, not yet, not yet.*

Same as you, I am just the sum of things I will never forget.

I Miss the Friday Train
and Have to Take the Monday Train

We pass by a town where the name of every place is three things:
*Tanning, Videos, & Laundry; Billiards, Beer, & Burgers; Guns,
Ammo, Pawn.* Twice, the blind woman sitting next to me squeezes
my knee and asks, "Are you still here?" which awakens a feeling I
had years ago looking at a line of industrial buildings in a parking lot
under the sun. Before I left for this trip, the first week of January, I
took the Christmas ornaments off the tree. I put them all on the
coffee table, and I looked at the bare tree until I was convinced that
it was the beginning of December, and I was about to put them all
on the tree. The conductor says that the train is already on
a two-hour delay, and I make a face like I see someone I know
outside the train, but they can't see inside. We pass straight through
the middle of Virginia, where the negative space around all the
missing girls in Charlottesville grows outward when I see the hesitant
burning of a car on fire in the rain. When I eventually realized that
the passenger next to me was blind, I knew for sure that she didn't
notice that I'd misread in the book I was reading, the word *unclear*
as *nuclear*. She says, "I still make my bed every day." No one in our
car has left the train yet; what if I'm the only one to leave the train?
What if everyone else has secretly agreed to stay on the train
together after they've dropped me off? She says she can still roll
a tight blunt. She'll never go back to Philadelphia, where she is
coming from, because her paralyzed friend made her cook all the
meals and walk to the store blind. Her friend didn't have any
furniture, "Just one wobbly kitchen chair and shit." Her hips hurt
the whole time. She gives me her credit card to buy her something
from the food car. I could do anything. "I can hear the hollow,"
she says, then asks if we are going through a tunnel. Once
I unexpectedly saw a person I loved in my hometown, and then my

hometown was no longer my hometown, just a place he was and then wasn't anymore. Whether or not anyone else noticed the change was unclear/nuclear. At my stop, I'm the only one, and it is likely that no one will notice me getting off the train, confirming I'm here. Maybe not even a person far down the road whose range of vision includes me and who is sitting at a red light with nothing to look at. It's a nice day outside the train. I hope I'll see a balloon somewhere or hear someone announcing something on an intercom far away. Though my car is in the parking lot, for a long time I stand outside facing the train station until I've convinced myself that it's a week ago, and I just got here with my bag, and I'm about to get on the train for the first time in a while, actually.

RFI (Request for Information)

Introduction

Because I am anxious that provocative
and meaningful coincidence is possible
and might elude me,

I am requesting the following information.

Background

As a child, desperate for resolution, I created
explanations. For every movie or story, my own *deus
ex machina* played in my mind, like a countermelody
to the plot, for the lovers or friends kept apart in the end
by dueling families, by betrayal or infidelity,
or most tragically by some unromantic interference.
After the credits rolled, I allowed them to sneak out
of the house, send penitent flowers, awake from death
and dreams. And all the unresolved difficulties that the
writers left wavering at the end of the story were just
accidents. Just unavoidable accidents, which were actually
ironic and humorous when you untangled the complications.

Objectives

- I need better associations and connectors.

- I would like to be able to categorize specific
  circumstances as either meaningful or arbitrary.

- All I want is for things to be explained.

Statement of Need

➤ A list of the four people on earth who look most like me

(My name called out loud in a place I have
never been, over and over, with no answer.)

➤ A list of unique utterances or thoughts of consecutive
   words which I have spoken or thought, which
   were spoken verbatim by someone else without my
   knowledge on any occasion, unique enough
   for the repetition to be significant.

(A narcoleptic in Louisiana saying, almost defensively,
without ever having heard of Descartes,
*There are no certain indications by which we may distinguish
wakefulness from sleep, that I am lost in astonishment.*)

➤ A list of unique utterances of consecutive words
   spoken by me and someone else at the exact moment,
   unknown to each of us.

(In our separate childhoods, Emily in Ohio and
me in Indiana, repeatedly quoting the
line, *I'm tired of going up the down staircase,*
on any occasion, coinciding.

A stranger on a train in Topeka as I am on an airplane
over Seattle in February thinking synchronously,
The sun on the daffodils outside the bay window . . .)

➤ A diagram which marks the lineage of all those, living
   or otherwise, who have come within two degrees of

separation from me, including in the first degree,
beyond acquaintances, encounters with strangers
whom I would remember if generously reminded.

(The little girl in Venezuela, singing in the kitchen.
The Miss America contestant who sat next to me
on an airplane who kept asking for more chocolate
and spoke of the pageant with embarrassment.
The anonymous boy in the store in South Bend.
His brothers or sisters. Any of their faces in this picture
of a crowd in a Sociology book I'm leafing through.)

> ➤ A spreadsheet of sums that reflect the frequency
> of my recalling the repetition of something arbitrary,
> significant to me only in its repetition.

(Some obscure catalogue, which you've seen twice
in other people's houses. Once in Canada.
The three-story, tudor-style house on Interstate 69
somewhere after Muncie, Indiana, a transgression
on the countryside, which I've passed four times, its
incongruous cross gables darkened by night, and which
appears in my thoughts, when I feel apprehensive.)

> ➤ A mailing list, with phone numbers, of all the people
> on earth, according to empirical evidence and under
> varying circumstances, with whom I would sustain
> the most meaningful, familiar, satiating affinity with
> enough imperfection to be complicated.

(I am taking my change from one of them now, at the grocery
store, in the only interaction we'll ever have. Would my

grandmother in South Bend, Indiana have been included
on this list? She died when I was five, before I could ever
ask her about our last day alone together, shopping for summer
clothes. Did she hear the music I heard, and had the melodies
in our minds been played out loud, would the chords have
layered into counterpoint, as the rain hurried us home?)

> ➤ Flash cards corresponding to everyone I will ever meet
> revealing the ways I will underestimate how they matter.

(The little boy in the store in South Bend whose mom
and siblings drifted to an abstracted part of my memory,
while he remained by himself, near me and my
grandmother, in the brief moment that he was an
anonymous boy who I would have forgotten forever.

The woman in the same store who looked just like
Suzanne Somers, which made her seem comically
harmless, her perfect blonde hair reaching her waist when
she leaned over to ask the boy his name, the counter-
melody pacifying my mind and negotiating that she was
his ironic and theatrical aunt playing a game they knew.

The cashier to whom the blonde woman said,
glibly, "He always does this," to deflate the boy's
desperate crying and protest, as she pulled the boy out
the front door, letting the disproportion into the store
the permanent absence which surrounded whatever
department to where his mother had wandered.

And her, the mother, resurfacing slowly to the front of the
store, her voice calling out his name, a repetition of whole notes,

[while another mother in Florida called out a different name concurrently, or in exact syncopation, or in a slower, sadder rhythm fifteen years earlier], the metronome of her voice recalling for me the cross gables, black narrow windows, and sloping roof, rising as recollection for the first time.)

I'll Never Get to Say

Silence tied the sheets into a winding knot—me
and you implicated in the dismantled pillow sham,
the bedroom fallow and still—I almost spoke,
interrupted by a gust of air; the window slammed
shut. Wyeth's Christina leaned in with that wind;
she pushed forward on the canvas one useless last time.

I threw in and folded; the last of the last. Time
was set on the longest cycle. It was not me,
but you who spoke first; the sheets began to unwind.
It wasn't your voice I heard, but some sham
version; your voice spoken to a stranger, slammed
repeatedly clean against me and shaken. I spoke

in tones thin as shoestrings caught in spokes—
tangled, hopelessly frayed, worn for the last time.
They caught and pulled, caused you to slam
to a stop, short of a defensive or precluding *not me*.
The quiet that followed grew stagnant, Havisham;
a hem moved rarely by will now, only by the wind.

I couldn't wish time in any direction but rewind.
But the air chilled and the leaves fell and the wind spoke
for us, pushed me aside, unnoticeable as an eyelash. Am
I to have wished for time to fast-forward instead, past the last time
we'd speak, to your future life with someone who was not me,
so I'd have known to listen harder before the door slammed?

I'd tried to decode acronyms you'd written: SLAM—
Sound Light And Motion, Space Launched Air Missile—to get wind
of whether you may have found Some Love Aside from Me.
I read every word as though they were words spoken

by you, for example Kundera's Tomáš, reading it for the last time,
". . . he had constantly had to hide things from her, sham,

dissemble, make amends . . ." I thought I saw the window sham
in the living room move when I'd slammed
the book closed on that page in my mind. The last time
we spoke, I barely heard your words underneath the wind
and I left fraught with the ones I never spoke
and with everything that was meant and not meant,

unsorted. It's a shame I'll never get to say, it was the wind
that slammed the door, after we spoke
for the last time, not me.

Excavating the Foundation

The sound of the steel hammer from the construction workers outside was his footsteps getting louder, harder; he was now ten feet tall, lumbering in and out of her fractured sleep. His arm on the creaky banister signaled a warning, his footsteps down the wooden staircase, a countdown. They'd been sleeping in separate rooms, so in the morning, she didn't see him, only heard, in her half sleep, his noises moving around the house. Outside, the workers ran the air compressor, which was the sound of him blowing all the evidence of their life together off the walls, the dust of their skin cells out the windows. In the bathroom, the water rushing from the faucet was an inlet to an ocean he was allowing between them. It ran for long enough to fill the hallway that led from him to her, fill her room—her bed against the wall, a peninsula. The door slam was shotgun fire. She imagined him outside on the walkway turning desolately back toward their front door. The construction workers put a jackhammer to concrete; he was spraying the door with bullets. Just before that, a bird that flew into the glass was someone throwing coils of rope that just ricocheted off the window, landing beyond her reach.

What Was Discovered After the Snow Melted

I tried to erase the wild honesty flowers growing along the highway
I'd driven hundreds of times, bury them in the blank drift of unmade
memories, so I could see the roadside the way I saw it covered in
snow, like I was driving away for the first time. The Everest climbers,
a woman and her husband, spent their third night above 8,000 meters
without oxygen. I read this in the newspaper at J's kitchen table on the
morning after our last night together. Months earlier, he said that if
he let me go it would be *in the gentlest way,* and I imagined ice slowly
breaking apart and into a river that flows beneath it or the soft landing
of a belaying rope into snow.

The first night I woke up next to J, he pointed out the window and
said, *Look at all the deer in the snow. Look.* I saw nothing. *Look,* he said,
pointing out the window right next to me, and I saw frost on the
glass, but beyond it there was nothing. When Francys was found by
other climbers, her gloves were thrown next to her. Her arms had
been removed from her jacket, her hat was off. Paradoxical undressing
is when a person with severe hypothermia will feel a sensation of
extreme warmth and begin tearing off her clothing. When I left the
first morning, he was on the front porch wrapping the dog's leash
around and around his hands, the snowflakes blowing in nervous
paths in all directions, each in a panic to find its way to the ground.
Don't leave me, Francys said, when they found her delirious from lack
of oxygen and unable to move. She was still fixed to the end of a rope.
Don't leave me, she said again, but they couldn't move her. The first
night, before not seeing the deer, he told me this shouldn't happen,
I shouldn't be here with him, but then he said *please be here in the
morning,* and in the morning I saw my clothes on the floor as though
I'd just found them there, unfolded like a note I shouldn't have seen.

They found Sergei's ice axe and rope near Francys. He'd returned
up the hill to rescue his wife and had fallen down the mountain face.
Before I drove away for the last time, I found, in J's driveway, a piece
of note I'd written months before. I could only make out the word
"mean," and I couldn't figure out in which sense it was meant, but I
felt every sense of the word at once. Significance, intention, a wrong,
an average. I added it to a list of things I've discovered in my lifetime
after snow has melted: an asphalt shingle that blew off the roof,
handlebars with streamers, a cloche hat. I wasn't allowed to wait for
the bus outside when it snowed, because one girl did, and they found
her body in the spring. At 30,000 feet, on a plane headed away from
J, I had a window seat. My mind stepped outside of the plane at that
height and felt the lack of oxygen. I began to imagine things I'd seen
him do, but way far away or way out of context or distorted, like him
saying *in the gentlest way* to the banker when he asks how he'd like his
cash or *please be here in the morning* to his reflection behind the frost
in the window. I stood back, like he told me to without saying, at the
impasse, where he kept falling under a tiring weight. I only held out
my hand, which led to all the rest of my skin, and was useful to him, I
think, like a soft sheet, tied into knots and let down. Useful, in feeling
his way out.

Chance

John sat on a park bench and, in the inhale that preceded a
weightless afternoon sigh, felt brightly that all of summer's agreeable
fragrances had come together in this very park, the way the pretty
girls in every high school all find each other, eventually, which led
him to recall how exotic was the elusive and nuanced collective scent

that trailed groups of girls in hallways, the vaporous
intimation like a mirage; though, if deconstructed, it could
also be identified as a fortunately chance blend of base oils
and their subtle overlying scents—jasmine, lotus, orchid—
plants in his mom's backyard.

Rachel and Erin met in the park years after their last meeting.
They exchanged versions of their recent lives and dispassionate
inquiries about old mutual friends who were buried in their thoughts
under the recent and the not-quite-recent, under thoughts of when
the mail would come and where the dog had buried his toys.

When John tried to catch Rachel's eye from the other side of a
netless volleyball match, Rachel was thinking about how she felt
small in that park, how she could feel the city miles to her left, and,
six hours beyond that, the last place she'd lived and what
was going on there without her.

Both John and Rachel thought the same rare thought at the same
moment, though, of course, neither would ever know. John,
however, felt a connection pass between them, which surged right
through what would have been a net serve, as they both thought, for
arcane reasons, the words of Catherine from *Wuthering Heights*:

*He's [She's] more myself than I am. Whatever our souls are made
of, it is the same.* And then each felt his and her unique history
of disappointments. All that Erin and Rachel had left in common,

immediately, were their sandwiches from the same shop.
So they talked about those.

In common also, however, between Rachel and Erin, was their
underlying, though unacknowledged hope, that everyone they'd ever
known they'd meet again, as though at an important reunion picnic
in the future, where the guest list revolved around each woman's
exclusive history and all the estranged lives of acquaintances would

hypothetically unite, so that both Erin and Rachel had let go
of everyone in her life, each time,
with halfhearted promises to retain them in her thoughts
and with only a tentative sadness. Today, however,
John, Erin and Rachel each felt that all their significant relationships

now seemed arbitrary. And despite that John saw another woman
twenty minutes ago and felt the same connection drifting through
the fumes of a family barbecue, and would again in five minutes and
again in five years with Rachel, under coincidental circumstances,
her hair dyed red,

the three of them felt, in the same moment, their hearts drop as the
weights shifted, the small, significant moving measure, one of many
which tipped the scales toward resignation and the resulting
sad freedom to love
less from now on.

This, they each felt later that day, while Erin, in an airplane,
saw a cloud and the whole shadow that it made from end to end
over the edge of the town below, and Rachel, shedding her
sunglasses and lifting her visor, drove into its shadow and then
from street to street in the shade.

A Disaster with Angie Telephone's Name on It

Naming things is only the intention to make things.

—FRANK O'HARA

Then they started getting really specific
with hurricane names, like Hurricane Kevin
Costner. And then a return of all my dreams where
I'm trying to outrun a hurricane and for some reason
dreams where little things don't work for anyone,
like all suitcase latches, for example, just stop working.
And words refuse to be read. The more I try to read them,
the further they retreat into a tinier and tinier font.
And I can't dream a yellow that's any more yellow than it is.
I try to dream it more and more yellow, but at some point
it can't go any brighter or deeper. At the same time, all the graffiti
that named people in bathroom stalls was evolving, becoming
relevant, having context. A bathroom stall in a gas station
off the highway in Indiana said, "Rose—I was here.
Where were you?" The top baby names that year were Pottery
Barn for a boy, Chipotle Grill for a girl. That day—the day the top
baby names were revealed, everyone waiting, watching
the news—there it was. Oh shit. Hurricane Angie
Telephone. People gave puzzled looks that specifically and
singularly asked, "How'd you get them to name a hurricane
after you?" As though I nominated myself or petitioned for a kind
of revisionist taxonomy of natural disasters for the sake
of self-promotion. As though a disaster with your name on it
ever unravels beyond the radar of recollection. "It was just random
and unnecessarily specific," I said, casually, "like Urban Outfitters'
Nature Contrast Sublimation Tank Top." "And all those sweaters,"
they continued seamlessly, "that all the stores named after girls
for a while in an obvious marketing ploy to make requisite and literal

the personalization of your closet—the Carrie Cardigan,
the Molly Pullover?" "Sure," I said, pulling nervously now on my
Angela Wrap-Around. Predictably, everyone thought that it was so
clever to play the Rolling Stones song. Everywhere I went, I was
trailed by news of my namesake's disaster and Mick Jagger
relentlessly grilling me: *Angie, Angie, when will those clouds
all disappear?* In every dream I'd outrun the hurricane or awaken
as it hovered above, mountainous ocean waves ascending
on either side of me. My dreams were now all being written
and directed by Lars Von Trier. The yellows became different
shades of yellow but never more yellow. My disaster followed
me like the last song I heard before sleep—waiting to play
in my mind every time I woke in the night. I couldn't see
the hurricane, but I could feel the rain. At times, crossing
an intersection, I've felt the phantom collision of a crossing
car pummel into mine and by the next stoplight pictured
the calamity all the way through to the cat, alone, meowing for food.
Now I imagine a roof blown off, taking the place of another roof,
someone's name displaced, taking the place of another name.
I impulsively bought out all the Angie Telephone Ribbed
Sequin Studio sweaters, keeping in mind of course that a sequined
sweater with your name on it will never disappear—will travel
the intended course of nature from rack to clearance bin to outlet
to ebay. I was spun all the way around on display, a rotisserie
in the window. I was disoriented. I wasn't sure whether
Easter had happened yet or not. As the storm gathered, I watched
it take a slight specific path through your house, submerging all
your important documents and whitewashing your favorite clothes,

lapping at your sliding glass door. And right before it left, it made sure your football team will lose this year. Because all that time you'd never said my name, and when we were in the car you stopped when Mick sang, *Angie you're beautiful*. I stopped singing there too. So, the hurricane played the episode of my naming over and over again on your TV forever. It was the 70s. My mom, either inexcusably undecided or reliably procrastinating, looked up at the nurse who held me out to her, the nurse who held her own name, Angie, always inside her somewhere, always coating everything in a light film of her name, always a refrain that harmonized on the low notes. "What will you name her?" she asked. My mom looked up at the nurse, back at me, back at the nurse again and asked, "What's your name?"

Call On Janus

Watching kids in a movie throw
water balloons from a rooftop,
my dad says, "As a game, boys
would climb the rooftops
in Beirut and shoot at passing cars.
One boy shot his father's car
by accident. Then he shot himself."

I call on Janus, the temple god who looked
forward and backward at the same time—
god of beginnings, doorways, transitions,
passages, endings—to provide the psychological
requirement of transition, painstaking, gradual process.

Oh, Janus, provider of hallways, purgatory,
intestines, creator of gyms in airports,
bestower of the sky as the sun is on
its way toward the apex of our portion
of firmament or away from it,
grantor of a star's descent, connect us more
seamlessly from image to metaphor.

Without you exists sudden shock, hypoxia
with weak pulse and clammy skin;
or an orphaned whale's attempt
to suckle a blue, slick-skinned yacht;
a departure with only a coat and a bag—no note.

While watching kids in a
commercial for laundry detergent
playing tug-of-war on TV, my dad
remembers the war in his hometown:

"In Beirut, they tied the right arm
and the right leg of a man to the back
of one car and his left limbs to the back
of another car, and then both cars drove
away, one east and one west."

Janus, bestow upon us the beauty
of the in-between that provides reprieve—
the fluttering and quivering
in the divide, coalescing
in the magnetic pull of retreat
and anticipation, illuminating
the before and after, pulling us
both ways at once.

Possibility

Because I imagined
possibility
there was a night under the stars

where I became distrustful
of gravity.
And felt myself ready

to move off by some force,
foreign and luring,
toward the uncontained universe.

I'm so sorry Tia,
about your brother.
Maybe he also imagined

possibility. Jumping
in the shallow
pond. I can see myself,

considering the dive,
water cooling my
ankles, so passive and lenient

that it would just lap and swell
beyond itself,
make an opening in

the ground for me.

Variable Expressions

I subtract the qualities reminiscent
of the mother from her daughter's face while
they stand behind me in line at the store,

and I conclude that the girl's father
is neither the deli clerk nor the evening
manager. The parabola of the girl's chin

is shifting because she is not allowed
to buy a candy bar, so I subtract years from
the mother's face and see her pouty and angelic;

her face as the sum of conflicting reactions rounded
to the nearest expression is approximately equal
to her daughter's. I divide influence and affectation,

and the remaining quotient is my face
in the rain when no one's watching, while I'm
thinking about his face, trying to quantify

the words there, though it is almost always left
blank or unsolvable. The store clerk has the faces
of two people I know in her own;

Danika's smile is appropriated
by this stranger and Tara's expression
of deference. Does the thought of them,

provoked by her likeness, make them nearer
or farther? The more she talks, the more
she adds her own angle—oblique questions

reflecting acute observation—the less distinct
the two faces. Two extracted primes absorbed again
into their composite. She talks about her day.

One face stays longer, then disappears.
I feel an exponential, equidistant lack
when I try to add their faces back.

Pretending to Be Asleep

is like knowing exactly what you
are saying to me, but nodding
yes, what else? anyway, as though
I have never heard what you are saying before.

I have to purify from my appearance
appraisal and purpose, my face
distilled to stillness. I have to guess
when to genuinely tremble,
never having seen myself in sleep,
moving aimlessly beneath
awareness I wager one hand
from the sheets, toward nothing.
How does one believably breathe?

It's like hearing words I was not
supposed to hear and just turning
in my chair as though I needed to reach
my arm this way, toward this phone,
toward anything, as if to say,
I am occupied; I was before.
It is all now exactly as I meant it.

I know that the blinds have just been turned;
I feel on my face a lighter darkness.
I cannot see whether or not you are looking.
And now, I don't know where you are at all,
only feel the painful paralysis
against the sheets, the pressing
presumption of parameters.

It's like entertaining the embarrassing
acquiescence that follows a reprieve,
the manic generosity and impulsive ease,
allowing the sharing of irrelevant secrets, even.

A roulette of movement shifts among light.
You could be any shadow.
I cannot bind my eyes tighter to contrive
absence. I loosen, rehearse an invention
on the other side of sight

that everything is not altered
with someone else
in a room.

Owen and Paul

It's any two strangers' conversation.
The proportions of the tall one's face
make him look like an Owen.
The other one easily a Paul.
Owen makes a face, a gesture
his forced half-smile squints one eye,
as he barely shrugs in a way that falsely
means *tentative*, in a way that pejoratively
leans and says, *I'll give you that much,*
a gesture which says entirely,
You know, it's like this. Maybe I'm wrong,
but it's something to think about.
The *maybe I'm wrong* suggested by some
softening of his eyes that kept him from
a face that said, *nice try* or *dubious.*

I catch my eye just beginning to imitate
the gesture, try it out in this coffee shop.
Maybe I'll start wearing this look after saying
things like, "Yeah, I'm pretty positive
that's the city rock 'n roll was built on."
Or after anything ending in, "most people
don't know that."

The face that Owen makes when he feels loss
is the same face Paul makes when he feels
empathy, I conclude without reason.
And that unintentionally, these expressions are false
annotations of what they've said or meant to say.

Owen and I are in a serious relationship
from across the coffee shop.
He thinks I mean something
I didn't mean. Something definitive.
It was the sun in my eyes or it was
the blinding rays of other wrongs
that preceded you, Owen.

He is constantly displaying a grin that I
deconstruct into microexpressions. I tell him
to hold that face in our kitchen or in line
at the movie theater so that I can
locate specific facial muscles
orbicularis oculi, masseter, temporalis.
I can't help it. He gives me the same
expression that Paul just got,
but without the *maybe I'm wrong*.

I wish I'd loved Paul first.
I try to look at him right now with
all the love I have.

His expressions are consolidated
into a neat package of closely associated
representations of emotion. Which I used
to mistake for apathy. Now I've learned
to live with my misunderstanding.

Owen's face gives him away.
And because of the proportion of, and spatial

relationship between, his features, I've read
love when he was one frontalis muscle
away. Turns out, often, he'd meant *pity*.

Oh, Owen. I've watched your face
all these years. Because a specific,
complicated sentiment
or combination of sentiments
is absent from your heart,
there are certain things
that your face cannot,
will never say.

Where Home Is for Now

There were only twenty minutes of driving
on paved road on the island of Koror, unless
you kept turning around and driving the same
road again and again or just drove right
into the Pacific. Living in Micronesia was like this.
I could smell plumeria trees before I reached them.

Driving home toward Ohio had seemed haphazard,
accidental like the Cleveland Art Museum.
Between Akron and Lake Erie, in a room of canvases,
Mary's dress was falling onto her arm in folds
of fragile stone over her skin. It was morning,
and I imagined that she had just dressed
her children, and, tying swift knots around their tunics,
she never wondered if the dead would live again.

I took route 50 past a Mail Patch Tobacco Barn.
These tobacco ads were painted on barns
by one person, who allegedly began each one
with the *e* in *chew*. I was driving next
to someone carried in a hearse;
I pretended we were both leaving Ohio
for the last time. I parted ways with the funeral
procession at Stroud's Run and then,
near Chauncey one car pulled to the side
of the road had lost its way to the burial.
The trees in the countryside were spare;
despite the forests, so many were alone.
Reflection and refraction through the

warm troposphere caused generous spaces,
silencing possible thunder.

Someone was standing against a wall with a map
tracing with his finger across the divisions
Textiles, Medieval, Abstract, Oceania. Every painting
made me want to cry or drink a glass of water.
Even when I looked at the framed landscape
through the window. So, in my pocket, I grated
two keys with one hand, dropped them,
and something seemed filled, and I waited.

Wherever I go, I cannot restore to my senses
the smell of plumeria in the air, no matter how
I try to recall it. Still, I envy the way a long road
can leave it all behind. How it casts off and forgets.
Even the road can't do this everywhere.

At a stop light, the funeral procession had passed
through a photo-enforced red light. As the cars
passed through without hindrance, the camera
flashed uncontrollably, like lightning.

So many paintings that it was overwhelming like
the burden of carrying everything
that I have loved with me everywhere I go.
I wanted to stop after three rooms and sit
in a French armchair from the eighteenth century.
But there was a rope tied around its arms.

Everywhere I am allowed the same few things,
temporarily. Like proportioning the sun's light with
the car visor until night resumes and I think of,
in the last room, a painting called *Lot's Wife*
railroad tracks filling the canvas from end to end.
I imagine watching my hands turn to grain on the
steering wheel, imagine tasting my mouth fill itself
with salt, the taste lasting just a second before I fall
into myself in a pile on the seat and grains of me fly
out the window, glinting into the sky with the stars,

then my car driving a little way on its own

and the lightning would be the way it is tonight
in faded flashes behind the clouds,
like it does not want to be seen,
but where else can it go?

In Paris, the Sun Is a Chandelier

said Caren, as we looked through the window of a pâtisserie;
the light was icing rows of macarons, meringues, petits fours.
The reflected columns from the portico of the building behind us
framed the desserts, making them administrative and legal.
A bike leaned against a telephone pole, its basket filled
with the reflection of crepes. A curtain blew open in an
apartment window behind us, spilling a pile of opera cakes.

We watched a man walking in the reflection—a line of meringues
went right through him.

We had eight hours in Paris. We searched for the Eiffel Tower
the way I continually search for people whose names are complete
sentences with intransitive verbs. Amy Burns, Justin Rose, Tom
Waits, Britney Spears. Or imperative verbs—I'd known a Claudia
Love; it was like she was always being urged to love.

On each of us, at least five different French perfumes from
perfumeries we passed along the way hung in the air with the feeling
that back home everything had stopped and waited for us to return.
I'd tried to make a sentence with the scents. A Scentence: "Opium,
L'air du temps." Which wasn't a sentence, more like a slogan.
All the scents named for verbs had evaporated. I added non
sequiturs on every pulse point:
Lady Million on my wrist, *Gold Medal* on my neck,
Weak behind my knees, *Je Reviens* on my ankle.

The scent I wanted didn't exist. It was sweet and floral, pacifying,
mawkish. The perfume in the air made me look for a door to open,
but we were outside.

I kept thinking about how soon we wouldn't be there.
Like when I'm lying next to some lover, I'm already thinking about

how soon we'll get up, and I'll no longer be lying next to him.
Or when I'm petting my cat, even when her purring is a plastic
accordion straw unbending, I'm thinking about how soon
she'll run off.

On the train, Caren looked up useful French phrases, like, *Je n'ai
rien fait. I didn't do it.*
Carrie had been in France a few months earlier,
and she left her *L'Ombre dans L'Eau*
for us right on the Seine.
Shadow in the Water in a beautiful bottle.

When Christmas came months later, the Christmas trees were all
too short, because we went to Paris and time stopped for us back
home.

We kept seeing the top of the Eiffel Tower and then it would
disappear for blocks. The probability of an event not happening
is equal to one minus the probability of the event happening.
Caren sprayed *Pi* in the air with *No. 5* and *Ce Soir ou Jamais!*
(Tonight or Never!)

The Eiffel Tower peeked over a building, saw us coming, then
ducked behind a high rise.

As we sat outside a café, Caren said something important,
and I'm putting this here as a placeholder until I remember
what she said. A man who was eating alone smiled to himself.

I thought of him at Christmas when I didn't have a Christmas tree.
Instead, I looked at the pine tree right outside my glass doors,
and I drew ornaments on the glass with permanent marker.
I thought, when Christmas was over, I'd just open the doors.

Red String Theory

*According to Chinese legend, the gods tie an
invisible red string—the red string of destiny—
around the ankles of men and women who
are destined to be soul mates.*

I am trying to will you from however far
away you are to step forward slightly so
that you and I, with the indefinitely long string
attached to each of us, will detain the man
who cut off this nice older lady on his way
into the building and then let the door slam.

Walking into my apartment today, the kids
outside of course jump-roped over the string,
limboed under it, and a policeman politely
asked if I would step around the corner
for just a minute so I might rope off the
area until some caution tape arrived. And
later I had to tie up the town strangler.
It was a long day, still not having met you.

This afternoon, I started crocheting the string
until I covered the western suburbs of Chicago
in one large afghan, shortening it considerably,
so I assume you ended up having to move
at least one city closer to here from wherever
you are. I hope the move went smoothly.

Waving to the birds, waving away clouds,
I tightroped on the string as high as I could,
higher and higher until behind me
I saw the thick red line of sunset, beside

me it was fading, and in front of me dark,
the sun unable to reach its arms all the way
around the earth; I went higher still,
to see if I could see you coming this way.

Below, I saw heads of men and women and the
strings connecting them across the round earth.
They were discarded cherry stems and pits tossed
into a bowl. I hear that the thread leading into
blind anticipation is better than a string of excuses,
a string of lies, one more string of disappointments.

In string theory, the string must be stretched
under tension in order to become excited.
I pull and give creating various tensions
so I can pluck a melody that I'll play (do you hear it?)
till there's too much pull on that end. Till we're caught
in a cat's cradle, till we go all the ways we're meant
and not meant to go, the string catching and tangling
in too many places to move us anymore.

Hoarders Cento

All lines taken from various episodes of the show "Hoarders"

Her emotional attachment is slowing down
the process. We're not making
decisions to think about it
later. I can hang it up,
put it on one of my mannequins. It turns
out that he's not the hoarder,
she is. You can celebrate

him without the items.
Your grief is holding you

back. When he died you were alone. It's ok.
The three-year-old wants to wipe things
down, he wants to sweep.
He will need to start identifying cognitive distortions.
It does get dark, I just get used

to it though.
Teapots, china, photographs, pictures.
There's a certain kind of postcard,
fabric, almost everything
in the world. I don't want to see
it empty; I can't stand it.
Leave those there. I'll go through
those; I'll go through all that.
He's waiting for bad things to happen,
and because he's waiting for bad things to happen,
worse things happen.
He does not appreciate

the peril he's in.
I've never stepped further

than here, than the front room.
By the time it became
obvious, there was nothing
anyone could do, including her.
She's been confined to one
room for five years.
I need that. I need
them.
Leave that there.
Before it all goes,
I'll go

through it all.

Ben's Face Is Saying Something
He Doesn't Want It to Say

Ben would have chosen the words
in his face more carefully, would have
included the word *dammit* in the movement
of his eyebrow, for example, had he known
that he'd been saying silently to Annie,
More and more I want to be alone.

Earlier, he didn't even have a chance
to ask her what he told her with his head
tilted tenuously, his arms innocuously withheld,
the voice in the room no one could hear
evicting them, edging them out.

Ben turns slightly from the window, now,
where the snow makes the quiet outside
equal to their quiet,
looks at Annie standing behind him,
the cat curled on the floor beside the chair,
making small, desperate noises in her sleep.

Ben is unaware of the muscles
lowering his eyebrows, the tightening
around the corners of his eyes.
He turns back to the window,
catches Annie's reflection
overlapping with his. He watches

cars drive through their temples, one
car skidding back behind their eyes,

their brows extruding branches, snow
driveling down their foreheads and over
their chins, and he conflates their two expressions.

He looks as though he has been discountenanced,
he believes. In the reflected wreckage,
he thinks that she is looking at him
as though she has come up short by so little
or as though *she is lost but somewhere close.*

But Annie is not looking at him. She is just
straining, with little tension, to see far down
the road, the snow concealing the wheat field
and falling to the farthest point she can see,
in the direction she will walk every day
after this, leaving that look in the window,
without saying where she is going.

How to Take a River with You

First, hundreds of years ago, name the rivers in and around West Virginia:

> Cheat River
> Lost River
> Mad River

And now the river is no longer water cutting through land, but, inevitably, ideas far removed from the actual river arise and someone from Colorado, or South Asia even, driving by, will make inferences and create a story about a River-namer who lost a poker match or conceded, surrendered to her betrayal, despite the way his wife looked in a specific red dress.

> (You know this, because driving through West Virginia, you imagined nothing short of a police sketch of the jilted or losing gambler's sad face as he christened each flowing body with a permanent disposition.)

Then have simultaneous or staggered memories involving one or more of the rivers.

> At a rest stop on the way to Florida in 1985, we'd forgotten to latch the car top carrier on top of our station wagon, and as we drove along the highway, my mother's dresses floated along as she ran (like Mad) up and down Lost River.

Then the resulting connotations from both the rivers' arbitrary names and the events involving them may be easily cross-referenced, creating various narrative rivulets and channels, and confluence of tributaries, which flow into a large body of human ideas, baptized into the stream.

For example, the connections are infinitely possible when,
because of their precarious positions to the edge, you
must make an unreliable decision between salvaging
your mother's red dress or blue dress.

Finally, you cannot divorce the river from any of this. You will try to
think of someone in West Virginia fishing in Cheat River in a southern
summer you thought of as one you'd never live in, the way you try to
imagine yourself as the same person with the name Tilly or Hattie.
And then you will live in that summer 25 years later, unexpectedly
and not remembering any of this for a while.

The dress, secured to the car by the rolled-up
window, waves like the car's sail along highway,
then is worn late to the evening service
in a one-room, pianoless church
in Florida. My mother, who taps her foot to
I've got a river of life flowing out of me,
feels the wet hem rippling at her knee.

Shifts

I.

From the table, I watch you and the TV after the cartoon movie
we have just watched: two blank screens,
as though you are trying to negotiate what has appeared *inside*
the TV and inside yourself, with the uneven lines of the world.

II.

I write my name in a notebook and don't want anyone
to see it there. So I draw around it, fill in spaces,
put a roof on it, and my name disappears
and turns into a house on a farm in the rain.

III.

I see myself walking to the door, turning my hand on the knob
and going out to the room where the guests are sitting, and they see me.
But I am still here, standing at the sink, drying my hands.
And now I step toward the door, the difference between alone and not alone.

IV.

I'm thinking of how the cartoonists
just shift one line in her face.
Just one line in her face,
and she shows cartoon sadness,
and then she cries big cartoon tears.

Now the Day Is Over

At my aunt's house, we sang
"Now the Day Is Over"
before bed, and I thought
we were the only ones
who knew it. I didn't know
what the word *nigh* meant,
but in my mind,
I pictured a cradle.
I didn't know what the word
sin meant, but in my mind,
I pictured a soldier. All the minor
notes we sang in the dark
made me feel everything
       I was missing.

The newspaper says,
"Woman in Iceland
Unknowingly Joins
Search for Herself."
She heard her own
description and it was
a resemblance she
couldn't imagine, long
eraser strokes softening
her temples, eyes drawn too
wide. She said, "No one ever

discovers me," and even when
she blew her own *cover*
                     she was *missed.*

When I look
at a missing girl's
child photo,
I don't know her,
but I feel like only
I know the nuances in her
face. Then I look at her
age progression picture,
and I feel panicked
at the image
of a blur of faces
in a crowd, looking.
I know she can't look
                     anything like this.

Red Full Moon

He drove right into the
red full moon, he said.
I imagined it was made
out of parchment paper,
held by cheerleaders,
everyone cheering on
the other side.

ACKNOWLEDGMENTS

Enormous gratitude to the editors of these journals where the following poems have appeared or will appear (sometimes in earlier versions):

Best New Poets 2008, "RFI (Request for Information)"; *Boston Review*, "Love and Containment"; *cellpoems*: "Red Full Moon"; *Cimarron Review*, "A Disaster with Angie Telephone's Name on It"; *Columbia Journal*, "Every Miss Universe Contestant Is From Earth"; *Conduit*, "Excavating the Foundation"; Dorothy Sargent Rosenberg Awards website, "Possibility"; *Drunken Boat*, "I Am Looking for You Here"; *Indiana Review*, "Index of Continuity Errors" and "There's No Face for This"; *The Iowa Review*, "Oh, My Kidneys"; *Lana Turner Journal*, "I Miss the Friday Train and Have to Take the Monday Train" and "People with No Sight Still See Ghosts"; *Narrative Magazine*, "I'll Never Get to Say"; *Nat. Brut*, "Dreamsickness"; *New Ohio Review*, "Owen and Paul" and "Pretending to Be Asleep"; *The New Republic*, "Chance"; *NOÖ Weekly*, "Aircraft Safety Information Pamphlet"; *Smartish Pace*, "Shifts"; and *Washington Square Review*, "The Woman Who Lives inside My GPS Directs Her Thoughts Inward."

First and fiercest thanks to Carrie Oeding and Kent Shaw for pushing me forward the most. I owe so much of this to you both.

Enormous gratitude also to Tara Williams and Eric Smith for the generous time they spent with these poems.

Endless gratitude to University of Arkansas Press for expertly turning this manuscript into a beautiful book, especially, David Scott Cunningham, Molly Bess Rector, Melissa Ann King, and Liz Lester.

Infinite gratitude to Jeremy Geddes for allowing me to use his painting, which was my dream cover long before it was the book's actual cover.

Thank you forever to these writer loves of my life: Caren Merz, Kristin Collins, Gregory Tolliver, Danika LeMay, Molly Fuller, Kristin Lillvis, Shanley Jacobs, Kirsten Clodfelter, Stacy Nielsen, Jona Colson, Caroline Chen, Tricia Gonzales, Melissa Burkhart, and Debbie Kennedy.

Thank you to these writers at Marshall; I felt so lucky to be there at the same time as you: Laura Sonderman, Mary Beth Ferda, Mary Barbara Moore, Rachael Peckham, Jessica Anderson, Daniel O'Malley, TJ Boynton, Daniel Lassell, and Cody Lumpkin.

Thank you for the valuable feedback, inspiration, and/or support of OU friends and colleagues: Ashley Seitz Kramer, Emily Zaborniak, Christine Adams, Jessica Cogar, Derek Robbins, Claire Eder, Katie Berta, Derek JG Williams, Emily Kramer, Megan Griffith, Lizzie Tran, Susanna Hempstead, Sarah Minor, and Devan Murphy.

Thank you to Susan Folger, Cory Gregory, Josh Wade Ferguson, Forrest Rapier and Emily Morris.

Generous thanks to my teachers—Jill Rosser, Mark Halliday, Eric Pankey, Jennifer Atkinson, Peter Klappert, Claire Bateman, Natalie Diaz, Kyle Dargan, and Rick Hill, as well as for support from Dinty W. Moore, Eric LeMay, and Paul Jones.

Eternal love and gratitude to my family—Winston and Jean Mazakis, Rob Mazakis, Liz Mazakis, Sue Ann and David Smith, David Mazakis, Ron and Mimi Moore, and especially to my brother Ric. I wanted to do everything you did. I wrote poems because you did.

NOTES

"Love and Containment" is for Caroline Chen.

The title "Every Miss Universe Contestant Is from Earth" was taken with permission from Ed Nelson's facebook status.

In "Dreamsickness," the words "but it's the lie of the beholder" were taken with permission from Michael Lizer.

"Possibility" is for Tia Tackett.